The Stereotypes and Prejudices Against the Homeless

In our judgmental society, it is all too common for individuals to make assumptions and hold biased opinions about those experiencing homelessness. These stereotypes and prejudices not only perpetuate the cycle of homelessness but also hinder our ability to address the root causes and find effective solutions. It is time to confront these misconceptions head-on and challenge our own biases.

One prevalent stereotype is that homeless individuals are lazy and unmotivated. This assumption fails to acknowledge the complex circumstances that can lead to homelessness, such as job loss, mental health issues, or family breakdown. The truth is that many people who find themselves without a home are victims of systemic failures rather than personal flaws. By perpetuating the idea that homelessness is solely an individual's fault, we ignore the structural and societal factors that contribute to this crisis.

Another harmful stereotype is that homeless individuals are dangerous or prone to criminal behavior. This unfounded fear only serves to isolate and marginalize those in need. In reality, the majority of homeless individuals are law-abiding citizens who are simply struggling to survive. By generalizing and stigmatizing them, we hinder their chances of finding stable housing and employment, perpetuating the cycle of homelessness.

Prejudices against the homeless also extend to assumptions about their hygiene and mental health. Society often assumes that homeless individuals are dirty, disheveled, or mentally unstable. However, these judgments fail to recognize the challenges faced by those without access to basic resources such as clean water, sanitation, and mental health services. Instead of labeling and ostracizing them, we should focus on providing support and resources to help them regain their dignity and stability.

To truly address homelessness, we must challenge these stereotypes and prejudices. We need to understand that homelessness can happen to anyone, regardless of their background or choices. By recognizing the systemic issues that contribute to homelessness and offering compassion rather than judgment, we can work towards finding long-term solutions.

It Is time for our judgmental society to acknowledge the harm caused by these stereotypes and prejudices. By educating ourselves and challenging our own biases, we can create a more inclusive and empathetic society. Let us come together to confront the judgmental attitudes that *perpetuate homelessness and work towards a future where everyone has a safe and stable place to call home.*

The Influence of Media in Shaping Public Perception

Subchapter: The Influence of Media in Shaping Public Perception

Introduction:

In today's modern world, media plays a pivotal role in shaping public perception on various issues. From politics to social matters, it has the power to influence the way people think, feel, and act. In this subchapter, we will delve into the significant influence of media in shaping public perception, particularly in the context of homelessness. As members of a judgmental society, it is crucial for us to understand the impact our media consumption has on our attitudes and beliefs towards homelessness.

Media Representation and Stereotyping:

The media has often portrayed homelessness in a biased and stigmatizing manner. Stereotypes are perpetuated, painting a one-dimensional picture of individuals experiencing homelessness. They are often portrayed as lazy, dangerous, or drug-addicted individuals. Such portrayals not only reinforce negative stereotypes but also create a hostile environment for those who are at risk of or experiencing homelessness.

Selective Reporting and the Power of Narrative:

Media outlets often choose to focus on extreme cases or dramatic stories, which may not be representative of the broader homeless population. This selective reporting can skew public perception, leading to a distorted understanding of the complex factors contributing to homelessness. It is crucial for us as a judgmental society to critically analyze the narratives presented to us and seek a more comprehensive understanding of the issue.

Influence on Public Policies:

Media influence extends beyond shaping public opinion; it also impacts public policies. The way homelessness is portrayed in the media has a direct impact on the policies and resources allocated to address the issue. Negative portrayals can lead to a lack of empathy and understanding, hindering progress in finding effective solutions to end homelessness.

Responsibility as a Judgmental Society:

As a judgmental society, we have a responsibility to critically evaluate the information presented to us by the media. By challenging stereotypes and seeking out diverse perspectives, we can broaden our understanding of homelessness. Media literacy and awareness can help us become more compassionate and empathetic towards those experiencing homelessness, ultimately driving positive change in our society.

Conclusion:

The influence of media in shaping public perception cannot be underestimated. It is imperative for us as members of a judgmental society to recognize the biases and stereotypes perpetuated by the media when it comes to homelessness. By actively seeking alternative narratives, questioning the information presented, and *advocating for fair and accurate media representation, we can contribute to a more informed and compassionate society. Let us strive to understand the complexities of homelessness and work towards ending the judgment and stigma that perpetuates it.*

The Role of Societal Judgment in Perpetuating Homelessness

Introduction:

In this subchapter, we will explore the crucial role that societal judgment plays in perpetuating homelessness. Addressed to a judgmental society, as well as those interested in understanding how individuals end up homeless, this section aims to shed light on the harmful consequences of prejudiced attitudes and highlight the importance of empathy and support.

Unraveling Preconceived Notions:

Homelessness is a complex issue that often arises from a combination of personal circumstances, systemic failures, and societal attitudes. However, a judgmental society tends to oversimplify the causes, attributing homelessness solely to personal failures or laziness. These preconceived notions perpetuate a cycle of stigmatization and hinder progress towards effective solutions.

The Blame Game:

When individuals are faced with homelessness, the judgmental society is quick to point fingers, often attributing their situation to poor decision-making or a lack of ambition. While personal choices do play a part, it is crucial to acknowledge the structural factors that contribute to homelessness, such as unemployment, unaffordable housing, mental health issues, and substance abuse. By solely blaming individuals, society deflects responsibility and fails to address the root causes.

The Impact of Stigma:

Societal judgment creates a hostile environment for those experiencing homelessness. It leads to discrimination in employment, education, and healthcare, making it difficult for individuals to escape the vicious cycle. Homeless individuals face a constant battle against societal stereotypes, which further marginalizes them and prevents access to opportunities that could help them rebuild their lives.

The Importance of Empathy:

By cultivating empathy, society can begin to understand the diverse array of circumstances that lead to homelessness. Empathy encourages individuals to question their biases and challenge societal norms, ultimately fostering a more inclusive and supportive environment. It is essential to remember that anyone can become homeless, and the circumstances surrounding homelessness are often beyond an individual's control.

Rethinking Solutions:

To address homelessness effectively, a judgmental society must shift its focus from blame to solutions. This involves investing in affordable housing, mental health services, addiction treatment programs, and job training initiatives. By acknowledging the systemic factors that perpetuate homelessness and working towards comprehensive solutions, society can break the cycle and offer individuals a chance to rebuild their lives.

Conclusion:

Societal judgment plays a pivotal role in perpetuating homelessness, trapping individuals in a cycle of stigmatization and preventing access to resources. By challenging preconceived notions, fostering empathy, and focusing on comprehensive solutions, a judgmental society can begin to dismantle the barriers that perpetuate homelessness. Understanding the complex factors that *contribute to homelessness is crucial if we are to build a more compassionate and inclusive society for all.*

Chapter 2: Understanding the Complex Causes of Homelessness

Economic Factors: Poverty, Unemployment, and the Wealth Gap

In this subchapter, we delve into the economic factors that contribute to homelessness, namely poverty, unemployment, and the widening wealth gap. By understanding these issues, we hope to challenge the preconceived notions held by our judgmental society and shed light on the complexities of homelessness.

Poverty, often regarded as the root cause of homelessness, is a multifaceted issue. Contrary to popular belief, poverty is not solely the result of laziness or poor decision-making. It is a systemic problem deeply ingrained in our society. Factors such as lack of access to quality education, healthcare, and affordable housing contribute to the cycle of poverty. Homelessness can be seen as the extreme manifestation of poverty, where individuals and families lack the means to secure stable housing.

Unemployment is another critical economic factor that leads to homelessness. Job loss, underemployment, and the lack of fair wages are major contributors to homelessness. In an ever-changing economy, job security is increasingly uncertain, leaving individuals vulnerable to financial instability. Furthermore, the stigma associated with unemployment often perpetuates a cycle of poverty, making it difficult for individuals to regain stability once they fall into homelessness.

The wealth gap, a growing concern in our society, exacerbates the issue of homelessness. The concentration of wealth in the hands of a few has widened the divide between the rich and the poor. As the wealthy amass more resources, the marginalized and vulnerable populations struggle to meet their basic needs. This wealth disparity perpetuates a system that keeps certain individuals trapped in poverty and increases the likelihood of homelessness.

It is crucial for our judgmental society to recognize that homelessness is not a result of personal failings, but rather a consequence of systemic economic factors. By addressing the root causes of poverty, unemployment, and the wealth gap, we can begin to create a society that supports and uplifts its most vulnerable members.

To end the cycle of homelessness, it is imperative for our judgmental society to advocate for policy changes that prioritize affordable housing, accessible education, healthcare, and job opportunities. We must challenge our own biases and assumptions, understanding that anyone can find themselves in precarious circumstances. Only through empathy, compassion, and collective action can we dismantle the barriers that perpetuate homelessness and create a society that truly supports and uplifts all its members.

Mental Health and Substance Abuse Issues

In the subchapter "Mental Health and Substance Abuse Issues" of the book "Homelessness Unveiled: Confronting a Judgemental Society Head-On," we delve into two critical factors that often contribute to homelessness: mental health challenges and substance abuse. By addressing these issues head-on, we hope to challenge the judgmental society and provide insights into how these struggles can lead individuals to become homeless.

It"is essential to understand that mental health issues affect people from all walks of life. However, due to various societal factors, those facing mental health challenges are often left vulnerable and unsupported, increasing their risk of homelessness. Issues such as depression, anxiety, bipolar disorder, schizophrenia, and post-traumatic stress disorder (PTSD) can impair an individual's ability to maintain stable employment and housing, leading to a downward spiral that ultimately results in homelessness.

Furthermore, substance abuse is another significant contributor to homelessness. It is crucial to acknowledge that addiction is a complex disease that affects people regardless of their socioeconomic status. Substance abuse can stem from various underlying issues, including trauma, mental health disorders, and societal pressures. As individuals struggle with their addiction, their ability to maintain stable housing and employment is severely compromised, often leading them to the streets.

By shedding light on the relationship between mental health, substance abuse, and homelessness, we aim to challenge the judgmental society's preconceived notions. Instead of blaming individuals for their circumstances, we encourage empathy and understanding. Homelessness is not a personal failing but rather a result of a lack of support systems and societal structures that fail to address mental health and substance abuse adequately.

To truly address and combat homelessness, we must prioritize mental health services and substance abuse treatment programs. By investing in these areas, we can provide individuals with the support they need to overcome their challenges and reintegrate into society successfully. This includes accessible and affordable mental health care, specialized counseling services, and comprehensive addiction treatment programs.

Ending the cycle of homelessness requires a comprehensive and compassionate approach. It involves acknowledging the intricate relationship between mental health, substance abuse, and homelessness and working towards providing individuals with the support they need to rebuild their lives. By confronting the judgmental society, we can create a more inclusive and understanding community that uplifts and supports its most vulnerable members.

Lack of Affordable Housing and Gentrification

Lack of Affordable Housing and Gentrification: A Dual Crisis Plaguing Our Society

In this subchapter, we delve into two interconnected issues that perpetuate the cycle of homelessness: the lack of affordable housing and the detrimental impacts of gentrification. As a judgmental society, it is crucial to confront these challenges head-on if we are to eradicate homelessness and create a more inclusive and compassionate society.

Affordable housing has become a scarce commodity, leaving many individuals and families without a stable place to call home. Skyrocketing rental and housing prices have resulted in a significant portion of our population being priced out of the market. This crisis disproportionately affects low-income individuals, who are forced to choose between paying for housing or meeting other basic needs such as food and healthcare. As a judgmental society, it is vital to recognize that homelessness does not arise solely from personal failures, but from systemic issues that perpetuate inequality and poverty.

Additionally, the harmful consequences of gentrification exacerbate the lack of affordable housing. Gentrification, often accompanied by urban renewal projects, can lead to the displacement of long-term residents and the destruction of tight-knit communities. As neighborhoods become revitalized, property values increase, forcing low-income residents out of their homes. The judgmental society often dismisses these individuals as "lazy" or "unmotivated," failing to acknowledge the systemic barriers that prevent them from finding stable housing. It is crucial for us to understand that homelessness is not a result of personal shortcomings, but rather a manifestation of larger societal failures.

To address these issues, we must advocate for policies that prioritize affordable housing initiatives. This includes the development of low-income housing options, rent control measures, and increased funding for housing assistance programs. Furthermore, we need to ensure that gentrification processes are conducted ethically and prioritize the well-being of existing communities. This can be achieved through community engagement, inclusive urban planning, and measures to protect residents from unjust displacement.

By understanding the root causes of homelessness and challenging our own judgmental attitudes, we can work towards a society that values compassion, empathy, and social justice. Together, we have the power to transform the narrative surrounding homelessness and create lasting change for those experiencing housing instability. It is time to confront these issues head-on and pave the way for a more inclusive and equitable society.

Family Dynamics and Domestic Violence

In this subchapter, we delve into the complex issue of family dynamics and its correlation with domestic violence within the context of homelessness. It is crucial for the judgemental society to recognize the intricate web of factors that contribute to homelessness, including the role of family dynamics and the devastating impact of domestic violence.

Many individuals who find themselves homeless have experienced tumultuous family relationships, often marked by abuse and violence. Domestic violence, a widespread yet often hidden problem, is a significant factor pushing people into homelessness. Understanding the connection between family dynamics and domestic violence is paramount in our journey to confront homelessness and challenge our judgemental society.

Domestic violence can occur in various forms, including physical, emotional, and sexual abuse. It is not limited to any particular socioeconomic background, race, or gender. It cuts across all sections of society, proving that homelessness can impact anyone, regardless of their circumstances. The judgemental society must acknowledge that it is not solely the fault or responsibility of the victim, but rather a reflection of a deeply rooted societal issue.

Family dynamics play a pivotal role in shaping an individual's trajectory towards homelessness. Many people who experience domestic violence may struggle to escape the cycle due to economic dependence, fear, or lack of support networks. The judgemental society needs to recognize that leaving an abusive relationship is not a simple solution, as victims often face numerous barriers including limited financial resources and inadequate housing options.

Furthermore, children growing up in households marked by violence are more likely to experience homelessness later in life. Witnessing domestic violence can have long-lasting psychological effects, often leading to a range of issues such as substance abuse, mental health problems, and a disrupted educational journey. Breaking this intergenerational cycle requires societal support and resources, rather than judgement and blame.

To truly confront homelessness, our judgemental society must address the systemic issues that perpetuate family dynamics leading to domestic violence. This includes providing accessible and affordable housing options, comprehensive support services for victims, and educational programs that promote healthy relationships. By fostering a compassionate and understanding society, we can create an environment where individuals feel empowered to break free from abusive situations and prevent homelessness.

In conclusion, family dynamics and domestic violence are intimately intertwined with the issue of homelessness. Recognizing the complexities and underlying causes of homelessness, including the impact of family dynamics and domestic violence, is crucial for our judgemental society. By confronting these issues head-on and providing the necessary support and resources, we can work towards ending the cycle of homelessness and creating a more compassionate society for all.

Chapter 3: Breaking Down the Myths: How to End up Homeless

The Domino Effect of Unforeseen Circumstances

In the intricate web of life, we often find ourselves caught up in a series of events that can lead to unforeseen circumstances. These circumstances can have a domino effect, toppling one aspect of our lives after another until we find ourselves in a place we never imagined – homelessness. This subchapter aims to address the judgmental society that often makes assumptions about how one can end up homeless, and offers a compassionate perspective on the underlying factors that contribute to this plight.

To the judgmental society, it is crucial to understand that homelessness is not a conscious choice made by individuals seeking to evade responsibility or live a carefree life. Rather, it is often the result of a series of unfortunate events that spiral out of control. It is easy to believe that homelessness only happens to those who are lazy, unmotivated, or have made poor life choices. However, life is much more complex than such simplistic judgments allow.

The domino effect of unforeseen circumstances can begin with a single event, such as a job loss or a sudden illness. Without the safety net of savings or support systems, individuals can quickly find themselves unable to pay rent or afford basic necessities. This loss of stability can lead to a cascade of challenges, including mental health struggles, strained relationships, and a loss of hope.

Moreover, it is important to recognize that not everyone has the same resources or support systems to fall back on when faced with adversity. Those who lack family or community support may find themselves more vulnerable to homelessness. Additionally, systemic issues such as lack of affordable housing, limited job opportunities, and gaps in social welfare programs can exacerbate the domino effect, making it even harder for individuals to regain stability.

Understanding the complexities of homelessness requires empathy and an open mind. Instead of passing judgment, society should focus on providing support, compassion, and resources to those in need. By addressing the root causes of homelessness, we can break the cycle of the domino effect and create a society that offers equal opportunities for all.

In conclusion, the domino effect of unforeseen circumstances can lead individuals down the path of homelessness. It is crucial for judgmental society to recognize that homelessness is not a result of laziness or poor choices but rather a complex interplay of unfortunate events and systemic issues. By fostering empathy and offering support, we can work towards ending homelessness and creating a more inclusive society that seeks to uplift and empower all its members.

The Spiral of Addiction and Its Impact on Homelessness

In this subchapter, we explore the intricate connection between addiction and homelessness, shedding light on the devastating consequences of this spiral. It is crucial for the judgmental society to understand that homelessness is not solely a result of personal choices or laziness, but often a complex web of circumstances, including addiction.

Addiction is a powerful force that can consume individuals from all walks of life. It does not discriminate based on socio-economic status, education, or background. However, it is important to acknowledge that addiction can be a significant contributing factor to homelessness. For those trapped in this vicious cycle, the spiral can be seemingly impossible to escape.

Many individuals experiencing addiction initially turn to substances as a means of coping with trauma, mental health issues, or overwhelming life circumstances. Unfortunately, the temporary relief offered by drugs or alcohol can quickly turn into a destructive pattern that erodes personal relationships, stability, and financial security.

As addiction takes hold, individuals often find themselves prioritizing their substance use over other essential aspects of life. This can lead to job loss, strained family relationships, and ultimately, the loss of a stable home. The constant need to acquire drugs or alcohol can quickly drain financial resources, leaving individuals unable to pay rent or maintain a safe living environment.

Moreover, the physical and mental toll of addiction can further exacerbate the challenges faced by those experiencing homelessness. The deterioration of physical health, coupled with the stigma surrounding addiction, often leads to isolation and further marginalization from society. Instead of judgment, what individuals enduring this struggle need most is empathy and understanding.

To end the cycle of homelessness, we must address the root causes, including addiction. It is crucial for judgmental society to extend a helping hand rather than harsh judgment. By investing in comprehensive addiction treatment programs, mental health support, and social services, we can provide a pathway to recovery and stability for those impacted by addiction and homelessness.

In conclusion, the spiral of addiction and its impact on homelessness is an issue that demands our attention and understanding. By recognizing the complex interplay between addiction and homelessness, we can begin to challenge the judgmental attitudes prevalent in society. Together, we can work towards creating a compassionate and supportive environment that offers hope and opportunities for individuals trapped in this devastating cycle.

Escaping from an Abusive Relationship: The Risk of Homelessness

In a judgmental society that often turns a blind eye to the realities of homelessness, it is crucial to shed light on one of the significant factors that can lead individuals into this desperate situation: escaping from an abusive relationship. This subchapter aims to explore the inherent risks faced by survivors of abuse when trying to break free from their tormentors, highlighting the critical role that society must play in providing support and resources.

For those trapped in an abusive relationship, finding the courage to leave is an incredibly difficult decision. The fear of retaliation, the financial dependence, and the emotional trauma all contribute to the complexity of escaping. Unfortunately, the path to freedom is often paved with obstacles that can lead survivors directly into homelessness.

When survivors decide to leave their abusers, they often face a sudden loss of financial stability. Many abusers control their victims' finances, leaving them without access to money or credit. Without financial resources, survivors struggle to secure housing, pay for basic necessities, or even afford legal representation. The lack of economic independence becomes a significant barrier that can push individuals into homelessness.

Furthermore, the risk of homelessness is exacerbated by the limited availability of shelters and transitional housing for survivors of abuse. These safe havens are often overcrowded, leaving many individuals without a place to seek refuge. The shortage of affordable housing options further compounds the problem, leaving survivors with limited choices and increasing the likelihood of homelessness.

It Is essential for society to acknowledge the interconnectedness of abuse and homelessness. A judgmental society often blames individuals for their predicament without understanding the underlying factors that led to their homelessness. Survivors of abuse need empathy, support, and resources to rebuild their lives and break the cycle of violence.

To address this issue, society must invest in comprehensive support systems that offer safe housing options, financial assistance, and counseling services specifically tailored to survivors of abuse. By prioritizing the needs of these individuals, we can empower them to escape the cycle of abuse without being thrust into the harsh reality of homelessness.

In conclusion, escaping from an abusive relationship poses a significant risk of homelessness for survivors. The judgmental society must recognize the challenges faced by these individuals and work towards providing the necessary support and resources. By doing so, we can create a society that not only confronts homelessness head-on but also fosters a culture of compassion, understanding, and empowerment for survivors of abuse.

The Impact of Natural Disasters and Environmental Factors

In our society, it is all too common to pass judgment on those experiencing homelessness. We often assume that individuals who find themselves without a roof over their heads have somehow brought this situation upon themselves. However, it is crucial to recognize the significant impact of natural disasters and environmental factors on homelessness.

Natural disasters can strike without warning, leaving devastation and displacement in their wake. Hurricanes, tornadoes, floods, wildfires, and earthquakes can destroy homes, livelihoods, and entire communities. These catastrophic events can push individuals and families into homelessness, uprooting them from the stability they once had. The loss of housing and possessions can be overwhelming, leaving many with no other choice but to seek shelter on the streets or in overcrowded temporary accommodations.

Environmental factors, such as climate change and pollution, also play a role in the rising number of people experiencing homelessness. As our planet faces increasing challenges, the most vulnerable among us are often hit the hardest. Rising sea levels and the destruction of coastal areas due to climate change displace countless individuals each year, forcing them to find new places to live or face homelessness. Additionally, the pollution of air, water, and soil can lead to health issues that affect an *individual's ability to maintain stable housing and employment.*

It is important to understand that anyone can fall victim to natural disasters or environmental factors. No one is immune to the devastating consequences they can bring. The judgmental society needs to recognize that homelessness is not solely a result of personal choices but often a consequence of circumstances beyond an individual's control.

By acknowledging the impact of natural disasters and environmental factors on homelessness, we can begin to shift our perspective and work towards a more compassionate and understanding society. Rather than blaming and stigmatizing those experiencing homelessness, we should focus on providing support and resources to help them rebuild their lives.

Ending homelessness requires addressing not only the immediate needs of those without homes but also the underlying causes. This includes advocating for policies that prioritize disaster preparedness and response, as well as working towards sustainable solutions to combat climate change and protect our environment.

In conclusion, natural disasters and environmental factors have a significant impact on homelessness. It is essential for the judgmental society to recognize that homelessness can happen to anyone and is often a result of circumstances beyond an individual's control. By understanding and addressing the root causes, we can work towards ending homelessness and creating a more empathetic and inclusive society.

Chapter 4: The Struggle to Regain Stability and Reintegrate into Society

Navigating the Shelter System: Challenges and Limitations

In our journey towards understanding and addressing homelessness, it is crucial to explore the challenges and limitations that individuals face when navigating the shelter system. By shedding light on these obstacles, we hope to challenge the judgmental society's preconceived notions and foster a more compassionate and empathetic approach towards homelessness.

One of the major challenges faced by those seeking shelter is the scarcity of available spaces. Homelessness affects a staggering number of individuals, and the demand for shelter far exceeds the available resources. This scarcity often leads to long waiting lists, forcing individuals to endure extended periods without a safe and stable place to call home. This limitation not only poses a *threat to their physical well-being but also hampers their ability to regain stability and reintegrate into society.*

Furthermore, the shelter system often fails to address the unique needs and circumstances of homeless individuals. Many shelters operate on a one-size-fits-all model, disregarding factors such as gender, age, mental health conditions, and substance abuse issues. This lack of tailored support can exacerbate the challenges faced by homeless individuals, making it difficult for them to access the specific help they require. It is essential for the judgmental society to recognize that homelessness is not a homogeneous experience and that a comprehensive and individualized approach to shelter provision is crucial.

Another limitation is the temporary nature of many shelters. While they provide immediate relief from the harsh realities of sleeping rough, the transience of these accommodations hinders long-term solutions. Individuals often find themselves moving from one shelter to another, lacking stability and continuity in their lives. This constant upheaval makes it difficult for them to address the underlying causes of their homelessness and find sustainable pathways out of this challenging situation.

Additionally, the shelter system is not immune to societal prejudices and stigmas. Homeless individuals often face discrimination and judgment from staff and other residents, making it a hostile and unwelcoming environment. This further isolates them from mainstream society and hampers their chances of reintegration. To truly confront homelessness, the judgmental society must confront its own biases and work towards creating shelters that are inclusive, supportive, and free from discrimination.

In conclusion, the challenges and limitations within the shelter system are significant obstacles that must be addressed if we are to effectively tackle homelessness. By acknowledging the scarcity of resources, the need for tailored support, the temporary nature of shelters, and the prevalence of stigma, the judgmental society can start dismantling its preconceived notions and work towards a more compassionate and solution-oriented approach. Only through collective efforts and a deep understanding of these challenges can we hope to create a society that provides sustainable solutions and supports all individuals on their journey out of homelessness.

Overcoming Mental Health and Substance Abuse Issues

In this subchapter, we delve into the critical topic of overcoming mental health and substance abuse issues among the homeless population. It is crucial for us, as a judgmental society, to understand the underlying factors that contribute to homelessness, including the complex interplay between mental health and substance abuse.

Homelessness is not solely a result of poor choices or laziness; it often stems from a combination of systemic issues, personal struggles, and limited access to resources. Mental health disorders and substance abuse problems can be both causes and consequences of homelessness, creating a vicious cycle that is challenging to break.

For those who find themselves on the path to homelessness, it is essential to address the root causes of mental health and substance abuse issues. Understanding the underlying factors that contribute to these challenges is crucial for developing effective interventions and support systems.

One significant barrier faced by individuals struggling with mental health and substance abuse is the stigma attached to these conditions. As a judgmental society, we must learn to empathize and offer compassion rather than judgment. By creating a safe and understanding environment, we can encourage individuals to seek help and support, thereby breaking the cycle of homelessness.

Overcoming mental health and substance abuse issues requires a holistic approach that involves access to affordable and quality healthcare, comprehensive mental health services, and substance abuse treatment programs. It is crucial to invest in resources and programs that address the unique needs of homeless individuals who often face multiple barriers to care.

Furthermore, it is essential to destigmatize mental health and substance abuse issues within our society. By promoting open discussions, providing education, and raising awareness, we can encourage empathy and understanding for those facing these challenges. This, in turn, will foster a more supportive environment that promotes recovery and prevents the further perpetuation of homelessness.

In conclusion, addressing mental health and substance abuse issues is a critical step towards ending homelessness. As a judgmental society, it is our responsibility to challenge our preconceived notions and stereotypes, and instead, offer support, compassion, and understanding. By investing in comprehensive healthcare and destigmatizing mental health and substance abuse, we can pave the way for a society that embraces all individuals, regardless of their struggles, and works towards ending homelessness once and for all.

Accessing Employment and Education Opportunities

In the subchapter "Accessing Employment and Education Opportunities" of the book "Homelessness Unveiled: Confronting a Judgemental Society Head-On," we delve into the reality faced by individuals who find themselves homeless and explore the pathways that can help them reintegrate into society through employment and education.

To our judgemental society, it is crucial to understand that homelessness is not a choice but a result of complex circumstances. By addressing the issue head-on and offering opportunities for employment and education, we can provide individuals experiencing homelessness with a chance to rebuild their lives and contribute positively to society.

One of the key pillars in ending homelessness is providing access to stable employment. Many homeless individuals possess valuable skills and talents that, given the right opportunities, can be harnessed for personal and societal growth. This subchapter emphasizes the importance of creating inclusive workplace environments that offer fair wages, training programs, and support systems to help homeless individuals overcome barriers to employment. By doing so, we break the cycle of homelessness and enable individuals to regain their independence and self-worth.

Education is another essential avenue for homeless individuals to access brighter futures. Unfortunately, limited access to education due to financial constraints or disrupted schooling can perpetuate the cycle of homelessness. This subchapter highlights the importance of implementing educational initiatives tailored to the needs of homeless individuals. Such initiatives may include flexible learning options, scholarships, and mentorship programs, ensuring that education becomes a viable pathway for them to escape homelessness and build successful lives.

By providing employment and education opportunities, we not only empower individuals experiencing homelessness but also benefit society as a whole. When we offer support and create an inclusive environment, we enable homeless individuals to develop their skills, talents, and potential. This, in turn, fosters social cohesion, reduces the strain on public resources, and diminishes the stigma associated with homelessness.

To the niches of "How to end up homeless," it is important to remember that this subchapter does not glorify or endorse homelessness. Instead, it seeks to shed light on the challenges faced by those who have experienced homelessness and to inspire compassion and understanding. By examining the pathways to accessing employment and education, we aim to encourage introspection and empathy, fostering a society where homelessness is addressed with empathy, not judgment.

In conclusion, "Accessing Employment and Education Opportunities" explores the vital role that employment and education play in ending homelessness. By offering inclusive workplaces, training programs, and educational initiatives, we create pathways for individuals experiencing homelessness to reintegrate into society, rebuild their lives, and contribute meaningfully. It is our collective responsibility, as a judgmental society, to confront the issue of homelessness head-on and provide the support necessary for individuals to regain their dignity and thrive.

Building Supportive Networks and Reconnecting with Family

In the subchapter titled "Building Supportive Networks and Reconnecting with Family," we explore the crucial role that supportive networks and family connections play in helping individuals facing homelessness rebuild their lives. This chapter aims to challenge the judgemental society that often dismisses the homeless as individuals who have intentionally brought about their own misfortune. By understanding the challenges faced by those experiencing homelessness, we can foster empathy and work towards building a more compassionate and inclusive society.

Contrary to popular belief, homelessness is not solely a result of poor choices or laziness. Many factors, such as job loss, mental health issues, domestic violence, or substance abuse, can contribute to someone finding themselves without a stable place to call home. Rather than condemning individuals for their circumstances, it is essential for society to offer support and resources to help them regain stability.

One way to address homelessness is by building supportive networks. These networks can consist of community organizations, churches, social service agencies, and volunteers who are dedicated to providing assistance and creating opportunities for those experiencing homelessness. By offering access to shelter, food, employment resources, and counseling, these networks can help individuals rebuild their lives and regain a sense of dignity.

Another vital aspect of addressing homelessness is reconnecting individuals with their families. Family support can play a significant role in helping someone escape the cycle of homelessness. By fostering open and non-judgmental communication, we can encourage families to embrace their loved ones who are experiencing homelessness and provide them with the support they need. Family reunification programs can facilitate this process by offering mediation, counseling, and practical assistance to help rebuild fractured relationships.

By actively engaging with individuals experiencing homelessness, society can challenge its judgemental tendencies and foster a more compassionate environment. It is crucial to recognize that homelessness can happen to anyone and that providing support rather than condemnation can make all the difference. By building supportive networks and reconnecting individuals with their families, we can help break the cycle of homelessness and create a society that values empathy, understanding, and inclusivity.

In conclusion, the subchapter "Building Supportive Networks and Reconnecting with Family" highlights the importance of addressing homelessness by offering assistance, resources, and a non-judgmental approach. By embracing empathy and understanding, society can work towards ending the cycle of homelessness and creating a more compassionate world for all.

Chapter 5: The Role of Government and Community in Combating Homelessness

Implementing Effective Housing Policies and Programs

In this subchapter, we will delve into the crucial aspect of implementing effective housing policies and programs to address the issue of homelessness. It is imperative for judgmental societies to recognize the importance of adopting comprehensive strategies that not only provide shelter but also empower individuals to regain stability and reintegrate into society.

To truly confront homelessness, it is essential to understand the underlying causes and complexities that lead individuals to end up without a home. By comprehending the factors contributing to homelessness, judgmental societies can then work towards implementing effective housing policies that address the root causes and provide sustainable solutions.

One of the key components of such policies is the provision of affordable and accessible housing options. It is crucial to prioritize the development of affordable housing units that cater to the diverse needs of homeless individuals, including families, veterans, and those struggling with mental health or addiction issues. These housing units should be integrated into communities, breaking down the stigma associated with homelessness and fostering a sense of belonging.

Another vital aspect of implementing effective housing policies and programs is the provision of supportive services. These services go beyond mere shelter and focus on addressing the underlying issues that contribute to homelessness. By offering mental health support, addiction counseling, job training, and education programs, judgmental societies can help individuals regain their self-sufficiency and prevent a cycle of homelessness.

Furthermore, collaboration between government agencies, non-profit organizations, and the private sector is crucial in successfully implementing these policies. By pooling resources and expertise, judgmental societies can create a holistic approach to combating homelessness. This collaboration can include partnerships with landlords, who can offer affordable rentals and support individuals transitioning out of homelessness.

Lastly, a comprehensive evaluation and monitoring system should be put in place to measure the effectiveness of housing policies and programs. Regular assessments will allow judgmental societies to identify areas of improvement, redirect resources, and ensure that the implemented strategies are achieving their desired outcomes.

In conclusion, implementing effective housing policies and programs is an essential step towards addressing homelessness in judgmental societies. By prioritizing the provision of affordable housing, offering supportive services, fostering collaboration, and establishing monitoring mechanisms, societies can make significant strides in ending homelessness. It is crucial to remember *that homelessness is a societal issue that requires empathy, understanding, and a commitment to providing individuals with the support they need to regain stability and dignity.*

Enhancing Access to Mental Health and Substance Abuse Services

In the subchapter titled "Enhancing Access to Mental Health and Substance Abuse Services," we delve into the crucial issue of addressing the challenges faced by individuals experiencing homelessness in accessing adequate mental health and substance abuse services. This chapter aims to enlighten the judgmental society and specifically those interested in understanding the complexities of homelessness and preventing it.

Homelessness is not solely a result of poor life choices or laziness. It is a multifaceted issue deeply intertwined with mental health and substance abuse problems. Individuals struggling with mental health disorders or substance abuse face a higher risk of homelessness due to a lack of access to proper healthcare and support systems. It is thus imperative for judgmental society members to realize that homelessness can happen to anyone, and compassion and understanding are essential in addressing the issue.

To effectively combat homelessness, we must prioritize enhancing access to mental health and substance abuse services. This entails investing in comprehensive and affordable healthcare programs that cater specifically to vulnerable populations, including those at risk of homelessness. By doing so, we can proactively address the root causes of homelessness and prevent individuals from spiraling into unfortunate circumstances.

Moreover, it is vital to eliminate the stigma associated with mental health and substance abuse. This stigma often prevents individuals from seeking help, perpetuating the cycle of homelessness. By creating an environment of acceptance and understanding, we can encourage those in need to seek the assistance they require and deserve.

Collaboration among various stakeholders is crucial in enhancing access to mental health and substance abuse services. Government agencies, healthcare providers, non-profit organizations, and the judgmental society must come together to develop comprehensive programs that address the unique needs of homeless individuals. This collaboration should encompass initiatives such as outreach programs, counseling services, and rehabilitation centers, which provide tailored support to those struggling with mental health and substance abuse issues.

By prioritizing the enhancement of access to mental health and substance abuse services, we can break the cycle of homelessness. This subchapter aims to enlighten the judgmental society on the importance of understanding the underlying causes of homelessness and tackling them effectively. It is only through compassion, empathy, and proactive measures that we can create a society that supports and uplifts its most vulnerable members. Together, we can confront the judgmental attitudes and work towards ending homelessness once and for all.

Fostering Collaboration between Nonprofit Organizations and Government Agencies

In the subchapter titled "Fostering Collaboration between Nonprofit Organizations and Government Agencies," we delve into the essential need for cooperation between these two entities to effectively address the issue of homelessness. This chapter aims to address the judgmental society, particularly those interested in understanding how to end up homeless, and shed light on the importance of setting aside prejudice and working together towards a solution.

Homelessness is a complex issue that requires a multifaceted approach. Nonprofit organizations and government agencies both play crucial roles in tackling this problem, but their collaboration is often hindered by misconceptions, bureaucratic hurdles, and a lack of understanding.

Nonprofit organizations, driven by compassion and a commitment to social welfare, often possess invaluable expertise and grassroots connections within the homeless community. They understand the unique challenges faced by individuals experiencing homelessness and can provide tailored support services, such as shelter, food, healthcare, and job training. However, they may lack the necessary resources and influence to enact systemic change.

On the other hand, government agencies wield the power to implement policies, allocate funding, and enforce regulations. They have the capacity to create long-lasting solutions by addressing the root causes of homelessness, such as lack of affordable housing, mental health issues, and unemployment. Nevertheless, they can sometimes be disconnected from the realities faced by homeless individuals and may struggle to implement effective strategies without the collaboration of nonprofit organizations.

To end homelessness, it is crucial for these two entities to collaborate and leverage their respective strengths. Nonprofit organizations can share their valuable on-the-ground insights, helping government agencies understand the challenges faced by the homeless community. By working together, they can develop comprehensive and sustainable solutions that address the needs of individuals experiencing homelessness while tackling the underlying issues that perpetuate this societal problem.

Collaboration can take various forms, such as joint task forces, information sharing, and resource pooling. Through these efforts, nonprofits can contribute their knowledge, experience, and expertise, while government agencies can provide the necessary funding, regulatory support, and policy changes.

By fostering collaboration between nonprofit organizations and government agencies, we can create a society that is compassionate, inclusive, and committed to ending homelessness. It is crucial for the judgmental society to recognize that homelessness can happen to anyone and that working together is the only way to bring about lasting change. Let us set aside our prejudices and join forces to confront this issue head-on, ensuring that no individual is left without a home or support.

Addressing the Stigma and Discrimination Faced by the Homeless

In our judgmental society, it is crucial to confront the stigmas and discriminations faced by the homeless head-

on. In this subchapter, we will delve into the misconceptions surrounding homelessness and explore ways to combat this judgmental mindset. By doing so, we hope to bridge the gap between those who have experienced homelessness and those who fear it.

One of the most prevalent misconceptions is the belief that anyone can easily end up homeless by making poor choices. While it is true that certain choices can contribute to homelessness, such as substance abuse or financial mismanagement, it is essential to remember that homelessness is often the result of a complex web of factors beyond an individual's control. Mental illness, job loss, domestic violence, or a lack of affordable housing are just a few examples of the many circumstances that can lead to homelessness.

To address the stigma, we must first challenge the notion that homeless individuals are lazy or lacking in motivation. In fact, many people experiencing homelessness work tirelessly to improve their situation and regain stability. By highlighting stories of resilience and determination, we can begin to shift the narrative surrounding homelessness.

Education is another crucial tool in combating discrimination. By providing accurate information and dispelling myths, we can foster empathy and understanding. Workshops, community discussions, and *awareness campaigns can all play a vital role in challenging societal biases and promoting a more compassionate approach.*

It Is also essential to examine our own biases and prejudices. Often, individuals find themselves judging the homeless without truly understanding their circumstances. By cultivating empathy and practicing active listening, we can learn to see beyond the stereotypes and truly connect with those experiencing homelessness. This personal connection can make a significant impact in dismantling judgmental attitudes.

As a society, we must also recognize the importance of providing support and resources to those in need. Investing in affordable housing, mental health services, and job training programs can help break the cycle of homelessness and empower individuals to regain stability. By advocating for these initiatives and supporting organizations that work towards ending homelessness, we can contribute to a more inclusive society.

In conclusion, addressing the stigma and discrimination faced by the homeless is a crucial step towards building a more compassionate and understanding society. By challenging misconceptions, promoting education, and fostering personal connections, we can work together to confront our judgmental tendencies head-on. Let us strive to create a society that values empathy, understands the complexities of homelessness, and actively works towards ending it.

Chapter 6: Empathy and Compassion: A Path to Change

Challenging Our Own Biases and Prejudices

Subchapter: Challenging Our Own Biases and Prejudices

In a society that often finds comfort in stereotypes and quick judgments, it is crucial to challenge our own biases and prejudices. This subchapter explores the importance of breaking free from preconceived notions, particularly when it comes to the issue of homelessness. By addressing the judgmental society head-on, we can begin to dismantle the misconceptions that perpetuate the cycle of homelessness and work towards creating a more compassionate and inclusive community.

The first step towards challenging our biases is acknowledging their existence. We all hold certain beliefs and assumptions, but it is essential to recognize when these biases cloud our judgment. The stereotype that homelessness is solely a result of laziness or poor choices is a prime example. By understanding that homelessness can be caused by a myriad of complex factors such as job loss, mental health issues, or domestic abuse, we can start to unravel the layers of prejudice that surround this issue.

It Is also crucial to confront the notion that anyone can easily end up homeless. While it is true that unforeseen circumstances can impact anyone's life, it is essential to understand the systemic factors that contribute to homelessness. By examining the unequal distribution of resources, lack of affordable housing, and limited access to mental health services, we can begin to challenge our preconceived notions and address the root causes of homelessness.

To truly challenge our biases, we must step out of our comfort zones and engage with the homeless community. By listening to their stories and understanding their struggles, we can humanize their experiences and gain a more empathetic perspective. This subchapter will provide practical guidance on how to engage with homeless individuals respectfully, avoiding stigmatization or further marginalization.

Moreover, this subchapter will delve into the importance of education and awareness. By educating ourselves and others about the complexities of homelessness, we can combat the ignorance that often underlies prejudice. Through increased awareness campaigns, community discussions, and grassroots initiatives, we can foster a more inclusive society that rejects judgment and embraces empathy.

Challenging our own biases and prejudices is not an overnight process but a continuous journey towards growth and understanding. By actively challenging our assumptions, engaging with the homeless community, and educating ourselves, we can dismantle the stereotypes that perpetuate a judgmental society. Together, let us confront our biases head-on and work towards a society that embraces compassion, empathy, and equality for all.

Volunteering and Advocacy: Making a Difference in the Lives of the Homeless

In a society that often judges and stigmatizes the homeless, it is crucial to challenge our preconceived notions and actively work towards creating a more compassionate and inclusive community. Volunteering and advocacy initiatives provide an opportunity to make a significant difference in the lives of those experiencing homelessness, while also addressing the root causes of this pervasive issue. By embracing these efforts, we can begin to dismantle the judgmental society we live in and create a more empathetic and supportive environment for all.

Volunteering is a powerful tool that allows individuals to directly engage with the homeless population, understanding their struggles and needs firsthand. Whether it is serving meals at a local shelter, organizing clothing drives, or participating in outreach programs, volunteering offers a chance to bridge the gap between society and the homeless community. By dedicating our time and resources, we can provide essential services and support, restoring dignity and hope to those who have been marginalized.

However, volunteering alone is not enough. Advocacy plays a vital role in addressing the systemic issues that contribute to homelessness. It involves speaking out against policies that perpetuate poverty and inequality, and actively advocating for affordable housing, mental health services, and job opportunities. By using our collective voice, we can challenge societal norms and push for long-term solutions that tackle the root causes of homelessness.

To truly make a difference, it is essential for the judgmental society to understand the complexities of homelessness. The subchapter "How to end up homeless" aims to shed light on the circumstances that can lead individuals to homelessness, dispelling common misconceptions. By examining the structural factors such as job loss, mental illness, domestic violence, and lack of affordable housing, we can challenge the notion that homelessness is solely a result of personal choices or moral failings.

This subchapter aims to educate the judgmental society and highlight the importance of empathy and understanding. By recognizing the shared humanity we all possess, we can break down the barriers of judgment and foster a society that uplifts and supports those facing homelessness. Through volunteering and advocacy, we can create a ripple effect of positive change, ensuring that everyone has access to the opportunities and resources they need to thrive.

In conclusion, volunteering and advocacy are powerful tools in combating homelessness and addressing societal judgments. By actively engaging with the homeless community, challenging systemic issues, and promoting empathy and understanding, we can make a tangible difference in the lives of those experiencing homelessness. Together, we can work towards creating a society that is defined by compassion, inclusivity, and justice.

Promoting Policy Changes and Social Justice

In this subchapter, we delve into the critical topic of promoting policy changes and social justice as a means to confront homelessness and challenge the preconceived notions of a judgmental society. It is essential for us to understand that homelessness is not solely an individual's failure or a result of personal choices; it is a complex issue deeply rooted in systemic failures and societal injustices.

To effectively address homelessness, we must recognize the need for comprehensive policy changes that prioritize social justice and equality. This requires a shift in our collective mindset, moving away from blame and judgment towards empathy and understanding. It is crucial to acknowledge that anyone can find themselves homeless, and it is not just a result of personal shortcomings.

One of the key steps towards promoting policy changes is challenging the stereotypes and misconceptions surrounding homelessness. By educating ourselves and others about the various factors contributing to homelessness, such as lack of affordable housing, mental health issues, unemployment, and systemic inequalities, we can foster a more compassionate and informed society.

To end homelessness, we must advocate for policies that prioritize affordable housing initiatives, mental health support, and job opportunities for marginalized communities. This entails holding our governments accountable for their responsibilities towards their citizens, demanding adequate funding for social services, and investing in long-term solutions rather than band-aid fixes.

Social justice plays a pivotal role in addressing homelessness and dismantling the judgmental attitudes prevalent in society. It requires us to challenge the systemic injustices that perpetuate poverty and inequality. By supporting grassroots organizations and initiatives that strive for equality and justice, we can actively contribute to positive change.

Furthermore, it is essential to engage in open and empathetic conversations with individuals who find themselves homeless. By listening to their stories and experiences, we can gain a deeper understanding of the systemic challenges they face and find ways to support them effectively.

In conclusion, promoting policy changes and social justice is crucial in our collective efforts to confront homelessness. By challenging stereotypes, advocating for policy reforms, and actively supporting social justice initiatives, we can create a society that is empathetic, inclusive, and actively works towards ending homelessness. It is only by confronting our judgmental attitudes and embracing social justice that we can pave *the way for a more compassionate and equitable society for all.*

The Power of Personal Stories: Humanizing the Homeless

In our judgmental society, it is all too easy to dismiss the homeless as faceless statistics or mere inconveniences. We pass by them on the streets, averting our eyes, and quickly turn our thoughts away from the harsh reality they face day in and day out. But what if we took a moment to listen to their personal stories? What if we allowed ourselves to be moved by their experiences, struggles, and dreams? This subchapter delves into the power of personal stories, urging us to humanize the homeless and confront our own judgmental tendencies.

Homelessness Unveiled: Confronting a Judgmental Society Head-On brings to light the hidden stories of those who have experienced homelessness. These stories serve as a powerful tool for awakening empathy and understanding within our judgmental society. By sharing their narratives, these individuals break through the barriers of stereotypes and challenge our preconceived notions about how someone ends up homeless.

The subchapter "The Power of Personal Stories: Humanizing the Homeless" introduces us to a diverse range of accounts from people who have experienced homelessness. They recount the circumstances that led them to lose their homes, providing an unprecedented glimpse into the complexities of their lives. From sudden job loss to family breakdowns, mental health struggles to unaffordable housing, these stories reveal the myriad factors that can contribute to homelessness.

By delving into these personal stories, readers gain a deeper understanding of the challenges faced by those experiencing homelessness. They come to realize that homelessness can happen to anyone, regardless of their background or circumstances. The subchapter tackles the misconception that homelessness is solely a result of laziness or a lack of ambition, highlighting instead the systemic issues and societal failures that contribute to this crisis.

Through these personal stories, the subchapter also aims to inspire action. It calls upon the judgmental society to confront its own biases and engage in meaningful dialogue about the roots of homelessness. By humanizing the homeless, we can begin to advocate for change and work towards solutions that address the underlying causes of homelessness. Only by truly listening to these stories and recognizing the shared humanity can we begin to dismantle the judgmental attitudes that perpetuate the cycle of homelessness.

"The Power of Personal Stories: Humanizing the Homeless" serves as a wake-up call to the judgmental society, urging us to challenge our preconceived notions and embrace compassion. By recognizing the power of personal narratives, we can foster empathy, understanding, and ultimately work towards ending homelessness.

Chapter 7: Creating a More Inclusive Society

Raising Awareness and Education on Homelessness

In a society that often perceives homelessness through a judgmental lens, it is crucial to confront these biases head-on and foster a deeper understanding of the complexities surrounding homelessness. This subchapter aims to raise awareness and educate the judgmental society about the realities of homelessness, as well as challenge preconceived notions about how individuals end up homeless.

The first step In raising awareness is dispelling common myths surrounding homelessness. Many believe that those experiencing homelessness are solely responsible for their situation, viewing it as a consequence of laziness or poor choices. However, it is essential to recognize that homelessness can be the result of a myriad of circumstances, including job loss, mental health issues, domestic violence, and systemic inequalities. By *illuminating these factors, we can shift the narrative away from judgment and towards compassion.*

Education plays a pivotal role in understanding the pathways to homelessness. Exploring the various ways in which individuals can become homeless is crucial, as it challenges the notion that it is solely a result of personal failure. Factors such as unemployment, lack of affordable housing, and inadequate access to healthcare can all contribute to homelessness. By shedding light on these systemic issues, we can inspire change and work towards preventing homelessness in the first place.

Additionally, educating the judgmental society about the consequences of homelessness is vital. Homelessness takes a toll on individuals' physical and mental well-being, making it incredibly challenging to break the cycle without support. Through education, we can foster empathy and encourage society to offer assistance rather than judgment.

One effective way to raise awareness and educate the judgmental society is through personal stories. Sharing narratives of individuals who have experienced homelessness can humanize the issue and challenge stereotypes. By hearing firsthand accounts, the judgmental society can gain a deeper understanding of the struggles faced by those without stable housing, ultimately fostering empathy and compassion.

In conclusion, raising awareness and education on homelessness is crucial in combating the judgment and stigma surrounding this issue. By dispelling myths, exploring the various pathways to homelessness, and sharing personal stories, we can challenge the judgmental society to confront their biases and work towards creating a more inclusive and compassionate society. It is our collective responsibility to dismantle the barriers that perpetuate homelessness and provide support to those in need, ultimately working towards ending homelessness altogether.

Supporting Affordable Housing Initiatives

Affordable housing initiatives are a vital component in addressing the issue of homelessness and providing stable, safe, and affordable homes for individuals and families in need. In this subchapter, we will explore the importance of supporting these initiatives and how they can contribute to ending homelessness.

One of the key factors that contribute to homelessness is the lack of affordable housing options. Many individuals and families find themselves unable to secure a home due to skyrocketing rent prices, limited availability, or discriminatory practices. This creates a vicious cycle where homelessness becomes a real possibility for those who cannot afford to keep up with the rising costs. By supporting affordable housing initiatives, we can break this cycle and provide individuals with the opportunity to secure stable and affordable homes.

Affordable housing initiatives encompass a range of programs, policies, and partnerships designed to increase the availability of affordable housing options. These initiatives may include the development of low-income housing projects, rent control measures, subsidies, and incentives for private developers to build affordable units. By investing in these initiatives, we can create more affordable housing options and increase the chances of individuals and families finding and maintaining a home.

Supporting affordable housing initiatives is not only a humanitarian act but also an economically smart decision. Studies have shown that providing stable housing reduces the strain on public resources, such as emergency shelters, healthcare services, and law enforcement. When individuals have access to affordable housing, they are more likely to maintain stable employment, pursue education, and contribute positively to their communities. This, in turn, leads to a stronger and more prosperous society for everyone.

To support affordable housing initiatives, the judgmental society must advocate for policies and legislation that prioritize the creation and preservation of affordable housing. This can involve contacting local representatives, attending town hall meetings, or joining advocacy groups that focus on affordable housing issues. By raising awareness and demanding action, we can ensure that affordable housing remains a priority on the societal agenda.

In conclusion, supporting affordable housing initiatives is a crucial step towards addressing homelessness and building a more inclusive and compassionate society. By investing in these initiatives, we can provide individuals and families with the opportunity to secure stable, safe, and affordable homes. It is time for the judgmental society to come together, set aside preconceived notions, and work towards ending homelessness by supporting initiatives that prioritize affordable housing for all.

Providing Accessible Mental Health and Substance Abuse Services

Subchapter: Providing Accessible Mental Health and Substance Abuse Services

In the battle against homelessness, it is crucial to address the underlying factors that contribute to this societal issue. Mental health challenges and substance abuse are two significant factors that often go hand in hand with homelessness. As a judgmental society, it is essential to understand the importance of providing accessible mental health and substance abuse services to those in need. By doing so, we can help individuals regain their stability and reintegrate them back into society.

One of the major misconceptions surrounding homelessness is that individuals choose this path willingly, believing they have control over their circumstances. However, the reality is far more complex. Many people experiencing homelessness have been grappling with mental health challenges, such as depression, anxiety, and post-traumatic stress disorder (PTSD). These conditions can make it incredibly difficult to maintain stable employment, relationships, and housing.

Moreover, substance abuse often becomes a coping mechanism for those struggling with mental health issues. Drugs and alcohol temporarily alleviate the pain and distress they experience, but eventually lead to a downward spiral of addiction and further exacerbate their homelessness. Breaking this cycle requires a comprehensive approach that combines mental health support and substance abuse treatment.

To end the cycle of homelessness, it is crucial to establish accessible mental health and substance abuse services. This means increasing funding and resources for mental health clinics, rehabilitation centers, and support groups. By offering a variety of options, individuals can find the help they need based on their specific circumstances and preferences.

Additionally, it is imperative to reduce the stigma associated with mental health and substance abuse. Our judgmental society often ostracizes and marginalizes those struggling with these issues, making it even more challenging for them to seek help. By promoting empathy, understanding, and education, we can create an environment that encourages individuals to seek assistance without fear of judgment or discrimination.

Furthermore, collaboration between organizations, government agencies, and communities is vital to ensure the effectiveness and sustainability of these services. Together, we can create a network of support that provides holistic care for individuals experiencing homelessness and struggling with mental health and substance abuse.

In conclusion, by recognizing the interconnectedness of mental health, substance abuse, and homelessness, we can work towards ending this cycle. Providing accessible mental health and substance abuse services is a crucial step in helping individuals regain stability, reintegrate into society, and ultimately end homelessness. As a judgmental society, we must confront our biases and strive to create an inclusive and compassionate environment that offers support and understanding to those in need.

Fostering a Sense of Community and Belonging

In a world often plagued by societal divisions and prejudices, it is crucial to acknowledge the importance of fostering a sense of community and belonging. This subchapter of "Homelessness Unveiled: Confronting a Judgemental Society Head-On" addresses the judgmental society directly, urging them to reconsider their beliefs and actions towards homelessness. Additionally, it aims to provide valuable insights and guidance to those who may be interested in understanding how homelessness can occur and how to prevent it.

It Is easy for people to fall into the trap of judging those experiencing homelessness without truly understanding the complex circumstances that can lead to such a situation. By fostering a sense of community and belonging, we can create an environment of empathy, compassion, and support, one that acknowledges the shared humanity we all possess.

To the judgmental society, it is essential to recognize that homelessness can happen to anyone. Life is unpredictable, and circumstances beyond our control can lead to financial instability, loss of employment, mental health issues, or familial breakdowns. By cultivating a spirit of empathy, we can move away from judgment and instead focus on creating a society that offers support and opportunities for those facing homelessness.

Furthermore, this subchapter aims to provide insights into the various factors that contribute to homelessness. By understanding the root causes, we can collectively work towards preventing homelessness from occurring in the first place. It delves into issues such as affordable housing, access to healthcare, education, and employment opportunities. By addressing these systemic issues, we can create a society that prioritizes the well-being and security of all its members.

To those interested in learning how to end up homeless, this subchapter offers an alternative perspective. By highlighting the devastating effects of homelessness, it seeks to dissuade individuals from making choices that may lead to such a situation. Through personal stories and case studies, it demonstrates the long-lasting physical, *emotional, and psychological toll that homelessness can have on individuals and families.*

Ultimately, this subchapter encourages the judgmental society to embrace a more inclusive and compassionate approach towards homelessness. By fostering a sense of community and belonging, we can collectively work towards dismantling the judgmental attitudes that perpetuate societal divisions. Together, we can create a society that prioritizes compassion, empathy, and support for all its members, leaving no one behind.

Chapter 8: Conclusion: Confronting Judgment and Building Empathy

Reflecting on Our Own Perceptions and Actions

In a society that often indulges in judgments and preconceived notions about homelessness, it is imperative that we take a step back and reflect on our own perceptions and actions. In this subchapter, we will delve into the deep-rooted biases that contribute to a judgmental society and explore ways to overcome them. By doing so, we hope to pave the way for a more compassionate and understanding society.

It Is easy to fall into the trap of believing that homelessness can only happen to others, and that we are immune to such circumstances. However, the reality is that anyone can end up homeless, and it is crucial to dispel the misconception that it is solely a result of poor choices or laziness. By examining our own beliefs and challenging these stereotypes, we can begin to understand the complex factors that contribute to homelessness.

One of the first steps towards combating judgment and prejudice is acknowledging our own privilege. Recognizing the advantages we have been afforded in life can help foster empathy and a willingness to extend a helping hand to those in need. Instead of turning a blind eye or blaming the homeless, we can embrace a mindset of compassion and actively seek ways to address the root causes of homelessness.

Another aspect to reflect upon is the role of societal systems and structures in perpetuating homelessness. By critically examining our own participation in these systems, we can identify opportunities for change. Are there policies or practices that contribute to the cycle of homelessness? How can we advocate for systemic reforms that address the issue at its core? These questions can guide us towards meaningful action.

Moreover, it is crucial to challenge our own biases and assumptions about homelessness. Engage in conversations with individuals experiencing homelessness, listen to their stories, and learn from their perspectives. This will not only help humanize their experiences but also broaden our understanding of the complex issues surrounding homelessness.

Reflecting on our own perceptions and actions is not an easy task, but it is an essential one. By taking the time to examine our beliefs, acknowledging our privilege, and challenging societal structures, we can contribute to a more inclusive and empathetic society. Let us strive to confront the judgmental tendencies within ourselves and work towards ending homelessness by fostering understanding, compassion, and meaningful change.

The Urgency of Change: Moving Towards a Non-Judgmental Society

In today's society, judgment has become an all-too-common reflex. We find ourselves quick to pass judgment on others, often without fully understanding their circumstances or empathizing with their struggles. Nowhere is this more evident than in our treatment of the homeless population. It is time for us, the judgmental society, to confront our biases and move towards a non-judgmental society that fosters compassion, understanding, and equality.

Homelessness is a complex issue that can affect anyone. It is not a choice or a result of laziness or bad decision-making. It is a symptom of systemic problems such as lack of affordable housing, mental health issues, substance abuse, and unemployment. By acknowledging this, we can begin to dismantle the stereotypes and prejudices that have plagued our society for far too long.

The urgency for change lies In the fact that any one of us could find ourselves homeless at any given moment. Life is unpredictable, and events such as job loss, medical emergencies, or family breakdowns can push anyone over the edge. By recognizing our vulnerability, we can start to develop empathy towards those experiencing homelessness and work towards comprehensive solutions rather than perpetuating the cycle of judgment.

To move towards a non-judgmental society, we must first challenge our own biases and misconceptions. We need to educate ourselves about the root causes of homelessness and dispel the myths that perpetuate stigma. By seeking out diverse perspectives and engaging in meaningful conversations, we can broaden our understanding and foster empathy.

Moreover, we must advocate for policies that address the systemic issues contributing to homelessness. This includes advocating for affordable housing initiatives, mental health services, and job training programs. By supporting these policies, we can create a society that offers a safety net for those who find themselves on the brink of homelessness.

In addition, we must prioritize community and compassion over judgment and exclusion. Instead of turning a blind eye or blaming individuals, we should come together as a society to support and uplift one another. This can be achieved through volunteering, donating to homeless shelters, or advocating for the rights of the homeless population.

The urgency to change our judgmental society is evident now more than ever. By embracing empathy, understanding, and equality, we can create a society that does not stigmatize or marginalize the homeless population. Let us confront our biases and work towards a more inclusive and compassionate world, where no one is judged for their circumstances but is instead offered support, understanding, and a chance to rebuild their lives.

Taking Action: What You Can Do to Make a Difference

In a society that often judges the homeless without understanding the complex circumstances that lead to their situation, it is crucial that we all take action to bring about positive change. This subchapter aims to provide guidance to those who may be part of a judgmental society, helping them understand how their actions and attitudes can contribute to ending homelessness. It also sheds light on the steps individuals can take to prevent themselves from becoming homeless.

It Is important to recognize that homelessness is not solely the result of personal choices or shortcomings. Rather, it is often the consequence of systemic issues such as lack of affordable housing, unemployment, mental health challenges, and addiction. By acknowledging this, we can shift our perspective and cultivate empathy and compassion towards those experiencing homelessness.

One way to make a difference is by educating ourselves about the root causes of homelessness. By understanding these factors, we can challenge our preconceived notions and combat the stereotypes that perpetuate judgment. Engaging in open and honest conversations about homelessness with friends, family, and colleagues can also help break down the barriers that prevent us from taking meaningful action.

Supporting local organizations that work tirelessly to address homelessness is another way to make a positive impact. These organizations provide essential services such as emergency shelters, hot meals, job training, and mental health resources. By volunteering our time or donating funds, we can contribute directly to these efforts and help provide a path out of homelessness for those in need.

Preventing homelessness among ourselves and others is equally important. Taking steps to secure stable housing, such as saving for emergencies, maintaining a support network, and seeking financial literacy education, can go a long way in preventing homelessness. It is crucial to remember that anyone can face unexpected circumstances that may lead to homelessness, and by taking proactive measures, we can protect ourselves and our loved ones.

By taking action to challenge our own judgments, support local organizations, and prevent homelessness, we can collectively make a significant difference. It is only through understanding, empathy, and compassion that we can truly confront the issue of homelessness and work towards a society that is inclusive and supportive for all. Let us rise above judgment and come together to create a society that values the inherent dignity and worth of every individual, regardless of their housing status.

Embracing Empathy: The Path to Ending Homelessness

In this subchapter, we delve deep into the power of empathy and how it can lead us to a society free from homelessness. It is a call to the judgmental society, urging them to shed their preconceived notions and embrace compassion.

Homelessness Unveiled: Confronting a Judgmental Society Head-On is a book that aims to challenge the widely held stereotypes and judgements surrounding homelessness. By addressing the root causes and societal factors that contribute to this issue, we hope to ignite a collective desire for change.

To the Judgemental Society, we understand that it may be difficult to comprehend how anyone can end up homeless. We often hear the question, "How to end up homeless?" This subchapter aims to provide insight into the various circumstances that can lead individuals onto the path of homelessness, with the ultimate goal of fostering understanding and empathy.

Homelessness can affect anyone, regardless of their background or previous circumstances. It is crucial to acknowledge that a series of unfortunate events, such as job loss, mental health struggles, or family breakdown, can push individuals to the brink of homelessness. By examining these factors, we hope to dismantle the judgmental mindset that often prevails.

To truly address homelessness, we must embrace empathy. Empathy allows us to see beyond the surface and understand the complex web of challenges faced by those experiencing homelessness. By putting ourselves in their shoes, we can begin to comprehend the immense difficulties they encounter daily.

This subchapter presents real-life stories and experiences, highlighting the humanity behind every homeless person. By sharing these narratives, we aim to break down the walls of judgement and foster a sense of compassion within the judgemental society.

Ending homelessness requires a multifaceted approach. It involves providing affordable housing, access to mental health support, and employment opportunities. However, none of these strategies can be successful without empathy. By embracing empathy, we can create a society *that prioritizes compassion and actively works towards eradicating homelessness.*

In conclusion, this subchapter serves as a plea to the judgmental society to open their hearts and minds. By embracing empathy, we can challenge the stereotypes surrounding homelessness and work towards a society that supports and uplifts those in need. Together, we can pave the path to ending homelessness and create a more compassionate world for all.